What Do Birds Say to the Moon?

In the summer of 1987, Joan Franklin Smutny taught me, then a young elementary student, to write free verse poetry in her Worlds of Wisdom and Wonder summer creative writing class. I have been writing poetry ever since. It has long been my dream to publish a collection of poems edited by Joan. This dream has now come true. Thank you, dear Joan, for a thousand years (and counting) of friendship, mentorship, and love.

What Do Birds Say to the Moon?

Handwritten inscription:
Becky + Stu –
Always be
inspired by
birds!

Kathryn Haydon

Poems

By Kathryn P. Haydon

Edited by Joan Franklin Smutny

SPARKITIVITY
NEW YORK

COVER AND BOOK DESIGN BY CHLOE LANDISMAN

ISBN: 978-0-9963856-0-2

Published by Sparkitivity Press
New York

Proudly printed in the United States of America.

For
Brad and Jeff

Contents

You have only your own pair of wings
And the pathless sky;
Bird, o my bird, listen to me,
Do not fold your wings.

- J. M. Tutt

What Do Birds Say to the Moon?

Morning: Blank Canvas

The songbird always sings before dawn.
Eerie darkness,
mind awash in shadows;
night streaks
speaking emptiness.

The songbird will sing.
Dark, dank
thoughts rumbling
through fitful sleep;
ghosts swirling a cold sweat.

The songbird will sing.
Hollow echoes
scratch your dreams
and nails screech
a looping chalkboard.

The songbird will sing.
Creeping fear

seeps through covers
flooding pillow,
drowning peace.

The songbird will sing.
Final faint stars
the opening measure
and slivers of
morning light, interludes.

The songbird will sing.
Orange glow
spreads across mind's horizon,
dissolving nightmares into
flat silhouettes.

The songbird is singing.
A dawn chorus of
hundreds, millions
erasing the night and
defending your right
to a new day.

Awake

Light

is perched on

tree tops,

with

the

birds

who

are

singing

"Good morning."

The Entertainer

He clings to the branch

with his wiry feet,

a red spherical seed balanced

proudly in his dainty beak

If I didn't know better

I'd say he had fastened on his

clown nose

and is about to perform

bird jokes to a crowd

of fellow black-capped chickadees

Nest

The instinct to protect,
to nurture one's young (love)
is woven into the nest.

The bird weaves in circles
(infinity's symbol)
no beginning, no end.

Fragile eggs are secure (safe),
lying-in the circle
of mother-love.

Cloud Dance

Today is the day
of the cloud dance
when they gather
around the leafless tree
careful not to touch,

like a cotton halo
that will dissolve on contact.
There they prance and signal
the hollow notes
that warn of winter's approach.

Today the tree is warmed
by the cumuli's song
but tomorrow it will
steady itself in bitter,
ruthless cold.

Gray Morning on the Pennsylvania Turnpike

Trees have shed their

party clothes.

Flowing gracious gowns that

sparkled in auburn golden light

lie crumpled

on the forest floor.

No shame, they stand erect —

      uncloaked by fog or foliage —

sleek, smooth-skinned bodies

proudly saluting

ephemeral gray sky;

nature's figure drawing models,

each curving branch

an outline of

uninterrupted creation.

Up close

strong and separate,

they link arms on the horizon,

together

lending softness to the hillside.

December Gray

A Pantoum

Halcyon winter lake is a
liquid stormy sky
an oyster shell cupping a pearl of fog
that spins an ambiguous spell.

Liquid stormy sky
steams ice crystals
that spin an ambiguous spell -
silver clouds, estranged from above.

Steaming ice crystals
at rest in perpetual motion are
silver clouds estranged from above
that shade the scene with smoke.

At rest in perpetual motion
whirlpools of dread
shade the scene with smoke
drawing clarity to the vortex of fear.

But whirlpools of dread
freeze in frigid air,
draw clarity from the vortex of fear,
and return mist to its lofty home.

Frozen in frigid air
the oyster shell no longer cups a pearl of fog
and returns mist to its lofty home.
Halcyon nests on winter lake.

January: Unseasonable

Autumn was detained this year

on her way out.

She did the job well:

stripped the trees,

painted the sky gray,

left fallow decay in her wake.

But she forgot to knock on winter's door.

A curtain of white, glistening purity

would be most welcome

to draw the shades of fall to a close

and move us beyond this perpetual November.

Winter Fowl

Chickens bide

their eternity

deep in your backyard,

alone with

their thoughts in

an ice-packed igloo coop.

They are content,

but when I call to them

they smile.

Hawk

The hawk perches
high in a tree
outside my window.

He doesn't know
I am watching him,
nor does he care:

I can't fly and
he's a fearless
bird of prey.

Thermometer
says below zero
yet he sits there

Sunbathing, like
it's a midsummer day.
Relaxed, ready to kill.

Silent Sound

Paper thin golden beech leaves are scattered like children's breadcrumbs along the snow path hewn by few boots since yesterday's snowfall. Artifacts of autumn, they lead us as a winding stream through the woods, frozen silent but for our crunching and the wind running its long fingers over stiff bare branches. A raven flies silently, but the forest feels deserted. No birdsong, no rustling brook. Trees stand unmoving, spiting the breeze. I lie flat on my back on the snow crust and stare up at the heavy sky. I hold my breath and listen to silence, frozen silence sculpted around me by the wind's ghost, the sky's tears, the chill in the air.

Past's Mirage

Hiraeth is a slow longing
that perpetually simmers
in your soul. It beckons you
to time and place that exist
only in rose-colored
nostalgia.

Hiraeth creaks
in wooden floor boards
draped with morning light;
it is a cat pawing at the rainbow
that crept in through prism glass,
untouchable.

Hiraeth wafts from
crisp fallen leaves
crunching beneath your feet
as they make their way
back into earth,
calling you back, too.

Hiraeth howls
like a frigid winter night;
it is the soothing,
crackling fire
on the opposite side of a
double bolted door.

Hiraeth is the tail
that we chase round and round,
the certainty of belonging
just out of reach,
the past rose-tinted
by wistful memory.

Rare

Four fiery cardinals

paused in an evergreen.

Yes, all at once

for at least twenty seconds -- still,

like ruby glass balls

glowing for Christmas.

I took it as a sign,

a gift

that shook me from

self-pitying gloom

and turned my thoughts

northward

to nod a quiet

thank-

You.

When the Moon is Full I

The moon

slipped into my bedroom tonight,

    without knocking.

He thinks I don't notice

but light puddles

on the carpet,

      narrow

      and

      long,

are whispering to each other

(as if I can't hear them)

    right next to my bed,

giggling and glowing Chinese lanterns

strung for a party

in the middle of the night

    in my bedroom.

When the Moon is Full II

The moon keeps sprinkling
poem dust on my pillows
and won't let me sleep,
sugar-coated poem dust
that tickles my thoughts
and teases them from rest.

What if my ceiling were glass
with only iron crossbeams
to deflect and define this
dazzling serenade?

He would sit with me all night,
gleams whispering
radiant word paintings
twinkling poem dust,
pied piper of dreams.

Dream, Interrupted

This morning
I tried to slip back into my dream.
It was warm in there, lighthearted.

The alarm squawked too early
and I wanted to know
what happened next.

Eyes closed, I slammed it off
so I could return to that place —
but the door had disappeared.

Radiance

"You're a beautiful shadow,"

        they say,

"dark cast of a tree,

branches and stems

spread regally upon the snow

and particularly stunning

on this perfectly moonlit night."

But they don't understand.

      I am a sun ray

      that the moon reflects

      and the tree blocks

      to create the elegant shadow

      by night and by day,

      I warm the earth

      I melt the snow

I am not the shadow, I am light.

Prism

The light offered me
  a gift this morning
   as I was dressing—
   rainbow parallelogram
    pausing on wood floor,
    just in case I noticed.
     I did, of course,
      and smiled.

The Photographs You Made in the Darkroom

a woman's body,
sideview,
interlocks with lapping
ocean waves

congruous creation,
curve
upon
curve:

hourglass hips
synchronize
with the arcs of
tree's smooth skin.

these curves, they are
desert sands sculpted by wind,
ribbons of light and shadow that
flow across snowscape,

the outline of treetops
where they meet the sky
and smoke that winds
its way above flames.

a fragile bud,
layers of fog,
a rippling lake:
curves are the thread that

interweaves creation,
the thread
of flawless
grace.

Blush Spring Soldiers

Magnolia tree has blossomed.

Her pink silken flags wave a ceasefire to winter,

even as buds in tall trees take cover in their shells.

The wind whipped up last night.

Today the ground is a battlefield littered with petals,

though most hung on proud and strong.

Cold stings my skin.

Before turning back for my woolen hat and down coat,

I salute the dauntless tree.

Reverence

Trees' blush-white blossoms
perch daintily on sunlight;

five silent psalms sheltering
the steadfast stream below.

Translucence bathes the soul of one
who pauses to perceive.

She felt stretched, taut; weights tied to each limb in an unrelenting pull. Her reservoir of purpose, so full just hours before, had evaporated into a puddle out of reach.

The sky was starless and black when she parked in the driveway and trudged up the walk lugging burdens with her laptop. Conversations played again in her mind, rewinding only phrases that gnawed at her vanished peace. Her feet dragged through thick mud, yet the earth was dusty, sucked dry by drought.

Unexpectedly, a low, consistent buzz found its way into the morass of her thoughts. Her eyes brightened as she saw him, the hummingbird in the dark. There he was, wings beating steadily above conical purple blossoms. So light, so swift, he sipped nectar from the ready florets.

The small, avian creature was merely quenching his own thirst. "But," she realized, "he's working for me, spreading pollen from flower to flower to blossom beauty in my yard." Here it was late, dark, and the ruby-throated one moved tirelessly, unburdened.

"Thank you, little bird," she whispered, as gratitude refilled her head and her heart. The reservoir was replenished, her purpose renewed. As lightness returned to her body and the burdens—heavy as they had been—fell away, she resolved to walk forward and press on making her own billowing mark on the world.

Mourning Cry

It took until noon

for me to understand.

The squawking bird-

I thought, "How odd

a seagull in the suburbs."

But now I know,

now I know.

The universal pain

of losing one's young.

Robin in the Road

One of the things
I love about springtime
is the birds.

Especially the elusive
orange-breasted robin
pecking for worms in dew-misted lawn.

He appears early,
foreshadowing leaves and blossoms
with a brush stroke of color in end-of-winter gloom.

Like a wise child,
he's skeptical of the passing stranger,
protected by staccato hops.

But today
he lingered just a moment too long,
tugging on his breakfast.

When I saw him
he was lying in the road draped by sunshine
on what should have been a carefree day.

It's only April,

and my robin's song is silent, much too soon.

He is lying in the road.

smiling,
ageless,
cradled in your
moment of pure elation.

You will always be joy

sparkling eyes
glowing face
incandescently happy.

You are the laughter

of a child
splashing in waves
running unbounded
on warm, sun-kissed sand.

You are the promise

whispered by spring's
first lavender crocus
suddenly appearing,
leaving winter behind.

You are the warmth

of moonbeams
slipping through
bedroom windows,
painting ribbons of light.

You are a songbird

confident that
dawn will arrive
even while enveloped in
silvery darkness.

You are the rhythm

of summer rain showers
gliding
down rooftops,
replenishing life.

In these expressions

of life,
of joy—
rebirth,

you will always be.

Nighttime From the Bay Window: A Nod to Seurat

Tall trees burst red buds
on horizon's canopy,
an impressionist's spring.

When moon backlights
platinum clouds,
ocean is sky.

Suspended at low tide,
the world tilts and
trees hang from earth.

Fleeting pointillism
mingles with shadows;
light-kissed sky fades to night.

Cloud Cover

I hope
the clouds come tonight
to play with you in your dreams
wrapping you in

white cashmere feathers
that fly you so high above
landfills and hardened fears
that you are

weightless wings
gliding like a glassy lake
fetterless,
free.

So I Took it as a Lesson

You were a friend
for several hours in
my night dream,
laughing, love-glow.

No familiar face,
no shape nor name;
just human,
defined by good.

You died then, and
they weren't sad
because they knew.
Their joy was mine, too.

Gentle Awakening

This morning
        I awoke
to bird voices surround sound -
open windows -
the leaves that are my curtains,
        singing.

Five Ways of Looking at Light

I.
Light is the
animus
that guides
the inner path.

II.
Perched on
windowsill,
light gently
warms you awake.

III.
Darkness
has no power
when faced with
a speck of light.

IV.
The light is
night's end,
unfolding
a new day.

V.
Light,
gift of sun,
shows earth
it is loved.

Morning at the Feeder

The birds wait for sunrise.
The birds wait
for sunrise. The birds
wait for sunrise.

The little birds
wait
and then they come
all at once,
vying for a perch.

But the bluejay descends.
The bluejay
descends. The
bluejay descends
and the feast
abruptly stops.

The following poems have been previously published:

"Morning: Blank Canvas" - Published in *Written River*, Issue 10, 2016

"Gray Morning on the Pennsylvania Turnpike" - Published in *Written River,* Issue 5, Vol. 2, 2014-2015

"Radiance" - Published in *Creativity for Everybody* by Haydon and Harvey, 2015

About the Author

Kathryn Haydon's poetry has been described as "healing, with the surprise of grace." Rooted in nature and joyful curiosity, she writes to uplift and inspire. Primarily a non-fiction writer, Kathryn is the author of *The Non-Obvious Guide to Being More Creative (No Matter Where You Work)* (2019), and co-author of *Creativity for Everybody* (2015) and *Discovering and Developing Talents in Spanish-Speaking Students* (2012). She is the founder of Sparkitivity, and a keynote speaker and strategist who helps organizations and schools maximize individual and collaborative creativity. An award-winning educator, Kathryn has written and spoken widely on creative learning and the secret strengths of outlier thinkers. She earned her BA in Spanish literature and economics at Northwestern University, and her MS in creativity and change leadership at the State University of New York. Please visit Kathryn at www.sparkitivity.com.

CPSIA information can be obtained
at www.ICGtesting.com
Printed in the USA
FFHW011508061118
49197935-53408FF